Lesson 1 ❤ COUNTED CROSS STITCH I

The materials required for counted cross stitch are few and inexpensive: a piece of evenweave fabric, a tapestry needle, some 6-strand cotton floss, and a charted design. An embroidery hoop is optional. All of these are readily available at most needlework shops.

Evenweave Fabrics

These are designed especially for embroidery, and are woven with the same number of vertical and horizontal threads per inch. Cross stitches are made over the intersections of the horizontal and vertical threads, and because the number of threads in each direction is equal, each stitch will be the same size and perfectly square.

There are three evenweave fabrics commonly used for cross stitch. They are:

Aida Cloth: A basketweave fabric in which horizontal and vertical threads are grouped, making the intersections for stitches very easy to see. Aida is woven with the intersections spaced in three different sizes: 11 count (11 stitches to the inch); 14 count (14 stitches to the inch) and 18 count (18 stitches to the inch).

The number of *stitches per inch* of any evenweave fabric determines the size of a design after it is worked. The photos in **Fig 1** show the same heart design worked on all three sizes of Aida. The more stitches to the inch, the smaller the design will be. Thus a design stitched on 18 count fabric will be considerably smaller than one stitched on 11 count fabric. Eleven count Aida is the best fabric on which to learn, as its intersections are larger and easier to see.

Fig 1

11 Count Aida

14 Count Aida

18 Count Aida

Hardanger Cloth: Woven with pairs of vertical and horizontal threads, the intersections in Hardanger are visible but not as pronounced as in Aida. All Hardanger is 22 count fabric (22 stitches to the inch), which makes the stitches very small and delicate **(Fig 2)**. Working on Hardanger becomes easier with practice.

Fig 2

22 Count Hardanger

Both Hardanger and Aida cloth are available in a wide range of lovely colors, but ivory and white are the ones most often used.

Linen: Evenweave linen is woven of single threads. Cross stitches are made over two threads in each direction. Linen is a bit difficult for beginners to use as there are no obvious intersections.

In addition to Aida, Har... other specialty fabrics available, in a wide variety of counts, colors and textures. There are evenweave ginghams; pillow squares with evenweave centers and stencilled borders; damasks with Christmas ornaments and dolls; even a wonderful evenweave ribbon-like trim, called Ribband®with a decorative edging.

There are also many completely finished projects with evenweave fabrics sewn right in: from baby bibs to towels to men's caps.

Evenweave fabrics are usually sold by the yard, half yard or cut in pieces. The per-yard price may seem expensive but a quarter of a yard provides enough fabric for many cross stitch projects.

Hoops

Counted cross stitch can be done with or without a hoop. If you choose to stretch the fabric in a hoop, use one made of plastic or wood with a screw type tension adjuster. You may use a hoop large enough to accommodate the whole design or choose a small hoop, whichever you prefer. Placing the small hoop over existing stitches will slightly distort them but a gentle raking with the needle will restore their square shape. Be sure to remove the fabric from the hoop when you have finished for the day.

Needles

Cross stitch is done with a blunt-pointed tapestry needle. The needle slips between the threads, not through them. The chart below will tell you which size needle is appropriate for each kind of fabric.

The higher the needle number, the smaller the needle. A needle becomes finer and shorter as the needle number goes up. The correct size needle is easy to thread with the thread specified for the project, and is not so large that it will distort the holes in the fabric. Threaded, the needle should easily slip through the fabric.

Special Note: Counted cross stitch kits often provide a needle that is too large for the fabric. Don't hesitate to change to a smaller needle.

Embroidery Threads

Cotton Floss: Any six-strand cotton embroidery floss can be used for cross stitch. The six-strand floss can be divided to work with one, two or three strands as required by the fabric. The chart below tells how many floss strands to use with the various fabrics.

FABRIC	STITCHES PER INCH	STRANDS OF FLOSS	TAPESTRY NEEDLE SIZE
Aida	11	3	24
Aida	14	2	24 or 26
Aida	18	1 or 2	24 or 26
Hardanger	22	1	24 or 26

The most popular brands of cotton floss for counted cross stitch are those that offer several hundred colors with many shades of each. These brands – and there are several available – use **color numbers** for identification. On charts, the colors are identified by numbers, and a key to the symbols used to identify each color is given.

Needlework stores have available interchangeable floss charts, so that if the chart is keyed to one brand, you can see what number to substitute in another brand.

The grandmother of all flosses is DMC 6-strand embroidery floss, and it is the DMC numbers which we use with the charts in this book. If you prefer to use another brand, don't hesitate to substitute.

Counted cross stitch is worked on washable fabrics, and is completely washable if you have checked the bleeding and fading of your colors first. The worst bleeders are reds, dark blues and purples. Test these before stitching.

Flower Thread: Usually imported, Flower thread comes in a variety of soft shades perfect for rendering subjects from nature. It comes in a matte or dull finish, and has a fine twist.

Flower thread is a little heavier than six-strand cotton floss: usually two strands of floss equal one Flower thread.

Other Threads: Other threads – such as metallics or fine pearl cotton – can be used to achieve special effects. Choose threads you like, but be sure they are fine enough not to distort the fabric, yet thick enough to provide good coverage.

Scissors

A pair of small, sharp-pointed scissors is necessary, especially for snipping misplaced stitches. You may want to hang your scissors on a chain or ribbon around your neck – you'll need them often.

Practice Materials

Here's what you'll need to practice Lesson 2:
7" square piece of 14 count Aida
Size 24 tapestry needle
2 skeins of six-strand DMC cotton floss,
    892 red and 517 dark blue
4" screw type embroidery hoop (optional)

Lesson 2 ♥ LEARNING TO CROSS STITCH

From the skein of red floss, pull out an 18" length and cut it off. Divide the 6 strands into 3 separate groups of 2 strands each. Thread 2 strands into the tapestry needle. Set needle and thread aside.

If you are going to use a hoop, center it on the fabric with the tension screw at 10 o'clock if you are right handed, or at 2 o'clock if you are left handed. Pull fabric taut and tighten screw.

If you are not using a hoop, fold fabric in half twice to find the approximate center.

Step 1: Because knots in embroidery show under the fabric when it's framed or sewn into a finished project, begin by using the "waste knot" method. The waste knot appears on the front of the fabric and is cut off when the thread from it is secured by later stitching. Make a knot in the end of floss and insert the needle from front to back of the fabric about a half inch below the fabric center. The knot will remain temporarily on the fabric surface.

Step 2: Bring the threaded needle up through a hole in the fabric about 5 holes **above** and 5 holes to the **left** of where it went in (**Fig 3**). Needle is now in position to make the first stitch.

Fig 3

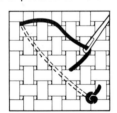

Cross stitch is done in two motions, bringing the needle up from the underside (which you have just done), then bringing it down again from the top side. This is called **stab stitching**.

Look at **Fig 4**. Where your needle comes up is the bottom left-hand corner of the first stitch, and is indicated by number 1. Now bring needle down through the hole at the top right-hand corner, indicated by number 2. Bring needle up again at 3, then down at 4. You have now made the first half of two stitches.

Step 3: To complete the cross stitches, bring needle up at 5, and down at 6 (**Fig 5**); then up at 7 and down at 8. You have now worked two complete cross stitches.

Fig 4

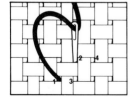

Fig 5

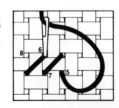

Step 4: Now look at the chart in **Fig 6**. Each **symbol** on the chart represents one **stitch** on the fabric. The two stitches you have just made are the top two stitches at the left side of the heart. Refer to the chart as you follow the next few steps.

Fig 6

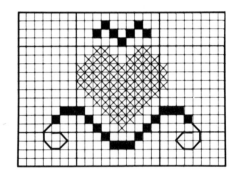

    ✕ = red
    ■ = blue
    — = blue backstitch

Step 5: Look at **Fig 7**. The next row of stitches starts one row below and one stitch to the left of where you have been working. Bring needle up at 1, down at 2; then work 3 more stitches in the same manner. Next on the chart is a blank square; this means the next space in the fabric is left unstitched. So skip that space and work 3 more diagonal stitches.

Fig 7

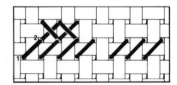

Now look at the chart (**Fig 6**). Above the last 2 stitches are 2 more stitches; in the next step you will move up and work the top two stitches.

Step 6: Following **Fig 8**, bring needle up at 1, down at 2; up at 3, and down at 4. Then as in **Fig 8**, cross these last 2 stitches.

Fig 8

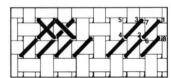

Step 7: This brings you back in position to complete the last cross stitch of the second row **(Fig 9)**: bring needle up at 9 and down at 10. Then work back across this entire row, crossing each stitch as you go.

Fig 9

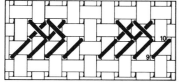

When the thread gets too short, finish off by turning to wrong side and running needle through the backs of stitches for about an inch; trim thread close to back of fabric. Thread the needle with another 18" length of 2 strands. Secure by weaving through backs of several stitches, bringing needle up where you need to begin.

Step 8: Now complete the stitching of the heart, working entirely from the chart **(Fig 6)**. Work from left to right across each row, then cross back from right to left. When the last stitch at the lower point of the heart is crossed, finish off your thread as before and trim close.

Starting a New Color

To embellish the heart, we'll work the top motif. Cut an 18" length of dark blue floss and again divide it into 3 groups of 2 strands each. Thread your needle with one group of 2 strands. Because of the irregular up and down steps of the crosses we will use a different technique than before: we will cross each stitch as we go, keeping the back as neat as possible.

Step 1: On the back of the fabric secure the new thread by weaving it through the backs of several heart stitches, ending at the top left stitch (the first stitch you took on the heart).

Step 2: The first space above the top left stitch of the heart remains blank (Fig 6). Work the first blue stitch in the next space above. Following the numbering of **Fig 10**, bring needle up at 1, down at 2; up at 3 and down at 4. Now, instead of working the crossing stitch from bottom to top in the usual manner, work it from top to bottom. Bring needle up at 7, down at 8. Continue across, following the number-

ing in **Fig 10**. As you work, think about what you are doing. This method of stitching gives a neater back, with no cross-overs of thread. After the last stitch is completed, run thread through stitches on back; trim thread close.

The Back Stitch

In stitching the bottom blue motif you will learn the **back stitch**. The back stitch can go vertically, horizontally or diagonally. It is always worked from hole to hole but can skip a space. Back stitching is usually done after all cross stitches have been completed.

In working the bottom motif you will continue to learn how to "plot a course" for your stitching. This means planning stitches so that the back of your work has only horizontal or vertical threads showing.

Step 1: Following the chart in **Fig 11**, anchor thread with a waste knot and bring needle up at 1. Numbers 1 through 14 will lead you through seven back stitches. Continue following the numbers for cross stitches until you have brought the needle down through fabric at 30. On wrong side of fabric, run thread under backs of last three stitches and bring needle up at 31. Continue following numbers until you have brought needle down at 54. On wrong side of fabric run thread under last three stitches.

Step 2: Now turn your work, and **Fig 11**, upside down (this is because we always try to work cross stitch from top to bottom). Begin again bringing needle up at 1, down at 2. Complete the motif, following the numbers. Finish off thread, trim close.

Special Note: Charts rarely give you such numbering to follow. It's up to you to study a design before you begin stitching, planning carefully where each stitch will go. Remember that you want to keep most stitches on the back vertical or horizontal, with few diagonals. It takes time and practice to learn to do this effortlessly.

Half Cross Stitch: The half cross stitch is exactly what its name implies: half of a cross stitch. The half cross can be worked either from right to left or left to right, but it goes over one space only. Unlike back stitch, half cross stitches are usually worked in rows along with cross stitches.

Fig 10

Fig 11

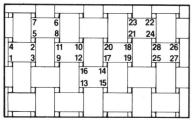

Bring Needle Up at Odd Numbers,
Down at Even Numbers

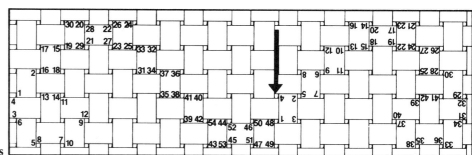

Lesson 3 ♥ WORKING FROM CHARTS

Charted – or graphed – designs are the key to counted cross stitch, for it is the chart that shows you just where to put each stitch. There are two types of charts: those printed in black and white, in which a different symbol is used for each floss color; and those printed in color, in which each different ink color represents a different color of floss. On any chart, **one square** equals **one complete cross stitch** on the fabric. Charts are usually accompanied by a color key which shows what color floss each symbol or color represents.

Charts can be foolers in one sense: **the size of the charted design is not necessarily the size that your finished work will be.** The work size is determined by the number of threads per inch of the fabric you select. For example, let's assume you're going to work a motif that is 22 stitches wide and 11 stitches high. If you are going to work the design on 11 count Aida (11 stitches to the inch), the worked design will be 2" wide and 1" high. If, however, you choose to work it on 22 count Hardanger, the worked design will be 1" wide and ½" high.

Lesson 4 ❤ PLANNING A PROJECT

After selecting your chart, determine the number of stitches in width and height of the design. (We always give you these counts with our charts, but other charts may require that you actually count the stitches in the design.) Next, decide which fabric you will be using and what its stitch count is. Divide the number of stitches in width of the chart by the number of stitches per inch of the fabric. This tells you how many inches wide the fabric must be for the design. Then do the same for the height. This is the formula:

sts on chart ÷ fabric sts per inch = size of fabric in inches

To the design inch measurements add enough fabric all around for a proper margin, at least 2″ more on all sides for use in finishing and mounting.

If your design is a small one, be sure to allow enough fabric to fit over your smallest hoop. The excess fabric can be cut off after stitching.

Cut your fabric exactly true, right along the holes of the fabric. Some ravelling will occur as you handle the fabric, however, an over-cast basting thread or machine zigzag will eliminate this, if it is bothersome.

Lesson 5 ❤ STARTING TO STITCH

First find the center stitch of the design. Often this is already indicated on a chart; if not, count to find it. Next, find the center of the fabric by folding it in half twice. You may wish to mark this center stitch with a cross stitch, which can be pulled out later.

It is best to start stitching at the top of the design (or the top of a color area) and work downward, whenever possible. This way your needle comes up in an empty hole and goes down in a used hole. This makes your work look neater and is easier than bringing the needle up through an already occupied hole.

To begin stitching, count up from the center hole of the fabric to the top stitches indicated on the chart.

You may wish to run horizontal and vertical basting threads that cross at the center. For a very large or complicated design, you can run a thread every 10 holes in both directions, forming a grid on the fabric that makes counting easier.

Things to Remember
- Never use knots – other than waste knots
- Anchor thread firmly at beginning and end
- Work designs from top to bottom
- Bring needle up in an empty hole, down in an occupied hole – when possible
- Never make jumps of more than four stitches, expecially if space between is unstitched
- Be sure all top crosses lie in same direction
- If you make an error, do not umembroider. Unembroidering can lead to snarls and tangles. If you have a large area to correct, bite the bullet and snip the mistake with the tip of your sharp scissors. For only a few stitches unthread the needle and use the blunt end to undo the mistake
- Trim thread ends close to back of work

At-A-Glance Reference Guide

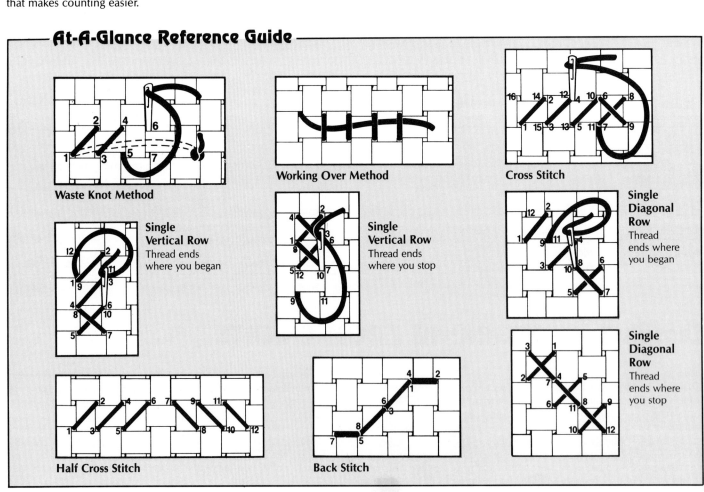

Waste Knot Method

Working Over Method

Cross Stitch

Single Vertical Row
Thread ends where you began

Single Vertical Row
Thread ends where you stop

Single Diagonal Row
Thread ends where you began

Single Diagonal Row
Thread ends where you stop

Half Cross Stitch

Back Stitch

Lesson 6 ❤ STITCHING ON CLOTHING

Cross stitch is a delightful decoration for clothing. Ready-made sweat-shirts, T-shirts, sweaters and dresses can become custom designs with the addition of just a few cross stitches. Children's clothing and household items such as curtains and table linens lend themselves beautifully to cross stitch.

In order to cross stitch on a non-evenweave fabric you need a grid to stitch over. Waste canvas provides that grid. Waste canvas looks like needlepoint canvas, but has two important differences. It is woven with parallel blue threads spaced exactly 5 stitches apart. These threads make the canvas easy to identify and provide a nice aid in counting. Waste canvas feels stiff when purchased but when dampened the sizing in it dissolves and it becomes very limp. The canvas threads no longer adhere to each other and can be pulled out from under the cross stitches – therefore going to waste!

Waste canvas is woven with double threads. Each cross stitch is made over two threads in each direction, as in **Fig 12**. When measuring waste canvas you will first count the number of stitches in each direction of the design you have chosen and then count two threads for each stitch in the canvas. Allow at least ½" extra canvas on all sides.

Fig 12

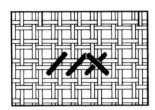

Figs 13-15 show how waste canvas is used. After canvas is cut, baste it to fabric **(Fig 13)**. Stitch entire design over the canvas on the top side and through the fabric on the bottom side. Be careful as you stitch that you go between canvas threads, **not through** them. When stitching is finished, wet canvas thoroughly with tap water. Canvas will become limp and slightly sticky. Begin at any corner and pull threads

of canvas out, one at a time **(Fig 14)**. Canvas threads will slide out from under the cross stitches. Once all canvas threads have been removed **(Fig 15)**, press stitched fabric on the wrong side. Your garment is now unique!

Fig 13

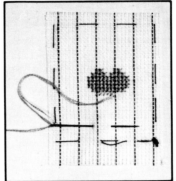

Canvas Basted to Fabric, Stitching in Progress

Fig 14

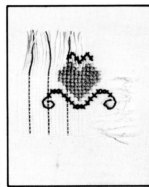

Stitching Finished, in Process of Removing Waste Canvas

Fig 15

Waste Canvas Removed

Lesson 7 ❤ STITCHING ON PERFORATED PAPER

Bookmarks, copies of antique samplers, and other delightful projects can be made on light-weight cardboard with evenly spaced perforations, called **perforated paper.**

Work on this paper just as you would on any evenweave fabric, but be very careful not to tear the paper. Work with a gentle tension and a fine needle.

If the unthinkable should occur, and you do tear the paper, cut a small piece from another sheet, place this underneath the tear, and stitch through two layers for a bit.

Lesson 8 ❤ STITCHING WITH BEADS

Small seed beads can replace stitches in the charted designs when using 14 count fabric. These small beads are just the right size for this fabric.

Step 1: A crewel embroidery needle, size #10, works well, but any needle that will fit through the bead hole can be used. Use two strands of ivory sewing thread or embroidery floss to match the Aida cloth. Since beads must be attached securely, use a small knot in end of thread.

Step 2: Bring thread through fabric to the front at 1, **Fig 16.** Pick up one seed bead with point of needle, and bring needle down at 2, the top right hand corner of the square. You are actually making a Half

Cross Stitch. To finish off, make a small knot on the back of the fabric and weave in ends.

Fig 16

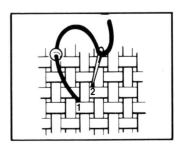

Lesson 9 💗 WORKING ON LINEN

To the experienced cross stitcher, linen is the ultimate fabric. It is the fabric on which to stitch heirlooms, or special gifts.

Evenweave linen permits the usage of a number of stitch variations, which gives greater flexibility to the designer. It has round threads, and comes in several different thread counts per inch. The most popular counts are 12, 18, 24 and 30 threads to the inch. It comes in bleached (white) or unbleached (a lovely creamy color).

Location of Selvages

In doing counted cross stitch on linen, a slight difference can be noted in a design worked with the selvages on the right and left and a design where the selvages are held at the top and bottom. The correct way is to have the selvages on the left and right vertically.

Using a Thimble

While no pushing of the needle is required to poke through the linen holes, a sewing stitch rather than a stab stitch is used on linen. Those who normally sew with a thimble will feel more comfortable wearing one.

Charted Designs

For linen work, one square of the design equals one cross stitch but the cross stitch is worked over two threads of the linen vertically (warp) and two threads horizontally (weft). See **Fig 17**. Often a darker line divides the grid into ten square sections (this could vary to be 12, 14, etc., but 10 is standard).

Fig 17

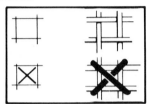

Square on Chart = 4 Threads of Linen

Lesson 10 💗 PLANNING A PROJECT ON LINEN

Determining Size

To determine size of your finished project and the amount of fabric required:

1. Count the number of threads per inch in the linen.
2. Divide this number by two (remember you are crossing over two threads with each stitch).
3. Now count the number of stitches (or squares) in the design, first vertically, then horizontally.
4. Divide each number of design stitches by the number of stitches per inch.

Example: The linen to be used is 28 threads per inch. Divided by 2 this equals 14. The design is 112 stitches (or squares) vertically. Divided by 14 this equals 8. The design is 140 stitches (or squares) horizontally. Divided by 14 this is 10. The image size is 8 inches by 10 inches. Add 6 inches to each measurement for hemming, turn over, or border. Cut the fabric 14 inches by 16 inches. If your arithmetic is doubtful at best, cut extra cloth. Even expensive linen is cheaper than your time. Waste a little fabric rather than waste your work.

Preparing the Fabric

A basting thread marking the center line can be an aid in counting. Start at a vertical thread (as shown in **Fig 21**), as you would for a cross stitch, and baste by two being sure not to deviate from the thread line. Repeat horizontally. It is then simple to count up 20 stitches or over 15, etc.

Lesson 11 💗 STITCHING ON LINEN

Hand position: Cup the left hand with finger slightly apart and relaxed. Now turn your hand over and place the cloth over the arched fingers with the thumb and index finger holding the cloth and the little finger anchoring it, as shown in **Fig 18**. Spread the third finger back from the index and thumb and work in this space or on the forefinger. On a tiny piece of fabric it may be necessary to anchor with the ring finger.

Fig 18

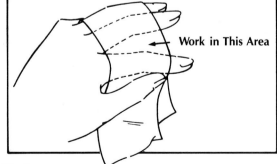

Work in This Area

Basic Rules

• Do not sew with fabric wrapped around one finger only. Use the entire hand, three fingers or at the very least two fingers to avoid distorting the fabric or having incorrect tension.

• Do not sew with the work on a table or in your lap but rather sit up straight and hold the embroidery at about eye level.

• An embroidery hoop is usually not used for linen cross stitching, therefore the stitches are made with a **sewing stitch motion**.

• The magic number for linen work is 2. The stitch crosses diagonally over two threads of the linen each way, as shown in **Fig 19**, up two, over two. Each square on the chart equals two threads of warp and two of weft, or to say it differently, count over two threads of the linen and up two threads for each square on the chart. **Count the threads of the linen, not the spaces.** Think of a ladder and count rungs not holes. This will be tedious but only for about three stitches. After that the eye begins to see in twos. Should a mistake occur – too many or too few threads counted – it will be immediately obvious by the slant, as shown in **Fig 20**.

Fig 19   **Fig 20**

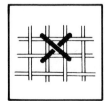 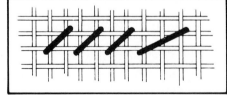

Starting to Stitch

Begin with a waste knot (see page 2). In placing the first stitch on linen, bring the needle up at a vertical thread as shown in **Fig 21**. Work a row of stitches by doing the understitches across, then the overstitches back, never by completing each stitch individually. The only exception is isolated stitches which can be completed individually. If you prefer, when working a vertical row of stitches, only one stitch wide, you can cross each stitch individually.

Never carry a thread over more than four threads of the open fabric (four threads equals two stitches). When the distance is greater than two stitches, end the thread and start again.

Work from the top, or center, of the chart down. In stitching, **stitch** each **stitch** from the bottom of the stitch to the top, but **work the design** from the top down. Why? When a needle comes up in an unoccupied (empty) space and down in an occupied (full) space, it will not ruffle the previous stitch. Therefore the results are the desired smoother stitches and the previously finished stitch is reinforced.

Fig 21

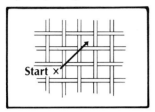

Start ×

Lesson 12 ❤ ADVANCED TECHNIQUES FOR LINEN

Scoring on Linen

Scoring is a great aid in hemming or marking the linen in order to space the design evenly.

To score, place the point of the needle between threads of the linen on the wrong side. With the forefinger of the right hand press slightly. Do not move this hand. With the left hand pull the fabric to the left. Keep the left thumb on the line of scoring, as shown in **Fig 22.**

Fig 22

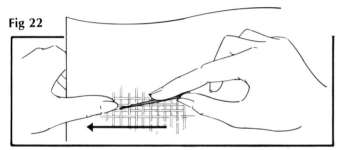

This is wrong side of linen. Needle remains stationary. Pull fabric left with left hand.

Stitching with Several Colors

If a design uses several colors in any area, it is useful to do the stitches of one color leaving the last stitch unfinished (work understitch only) and then bring the thread which is on the front side of the fabric up and to the side, out of the way of stitching, temporarily. Do the next color in the same way using another needle, and the next, etc. See **Fig 23.** When a previously used color is required run the thread of that color through the intervening stitches to the new area.

Fig 23

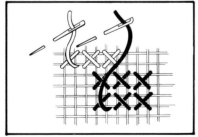

Use this technique discreetly, such as for areas of intricate shading. Remember the best work will have mostly vertical lines on the reverse.

Stitch Variations

Linen, because it provides four threads of background fabric per stitch, allows a certain flexibility in the stitches themselves. Standard stitch variations include the ¾ stitch and the backstitch.

The ¾ stitch will be indicated on a chart as a color symbol filling half the square, as shown in **Fig 24**. The long stitch is the overstitch even when the direction is opposite the other overstitches (in order to carry out the design requirements). "Teasing stitches" make possible designs that incorporate tiny noses for small figures, trailing leaves in a small plant design, more true roundness where roundness is needed.

Teasing Stitches

Fig 24

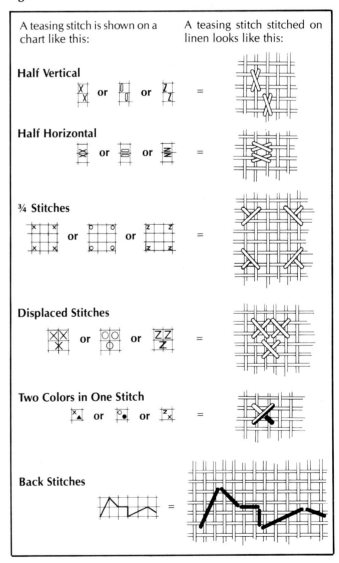

A teasing stitch is shown on a chart like this:	A teasing stitch stitched on linen looks like this:
Half Vertical	
Half Horizontal	
¾ Stitches	
Displaced Stitches	
Two Colors in One Stitch	
Back Stitches	

Specific instructions for finishing projects photographed on the back cover are on page 18.

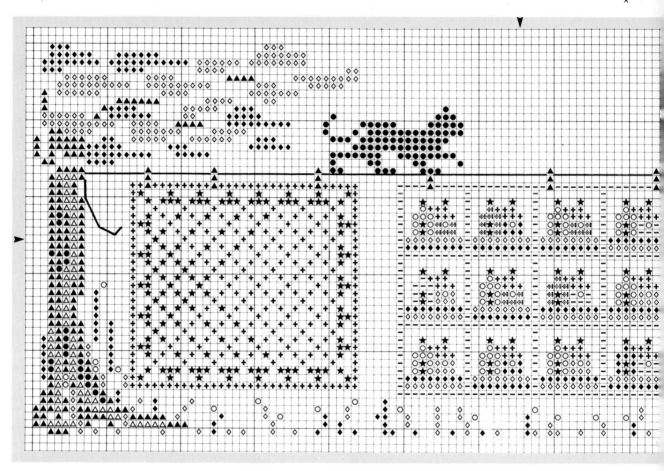

♡ ALPHABETS ──────────────────

Use these alphabets for charting any message, or personalize your stitchery with the date and your initials. The backstitch alphabet was used for the "Happy Birthday Bookmark" photographed on the back cover. It was stitched on 14 count ivory Aida cloth using the practice Heart design charted on page 2. See "Finishing Cross Stitch Bookmark," page 17.

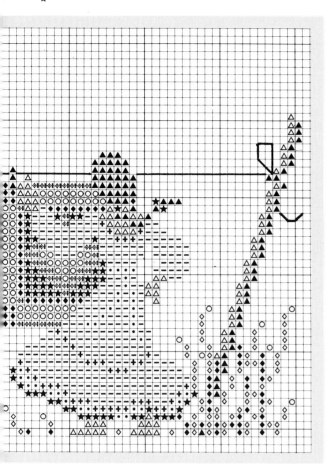

Quilter's Helper

design area 131 sts wide × 51 sts high

Color Key

- • = white
- ★ = 666 red
- O = 742 gold
- − = 996 lt blue
- + = 797 dk blue
- ✤ = 550 purple
- ◇ = 703 lt green
- ◆ = 699 dk green
- △ = 758 tan
- ▲ = 400 brown
- ● = 310 black
- ╱ = brown backstitch

The "Quilter's Helper," as photographed on the back cover, was stitched on 14 count ivory Aida cloth and finished in a 14" × 8" frame. See "Finishing Cross Stitch for Framing," page 17.

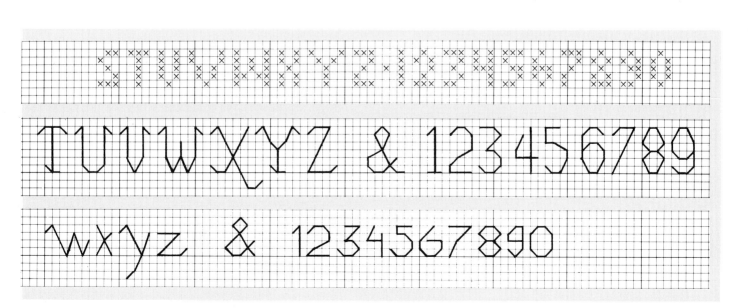

The "Carousel Charmers," as photographed on the back cover, were stitched on 14 count ivory Aida cloth and finished in 5" embroidery hoops. See "Finishing Cross Stitch in Hoop," page 17.

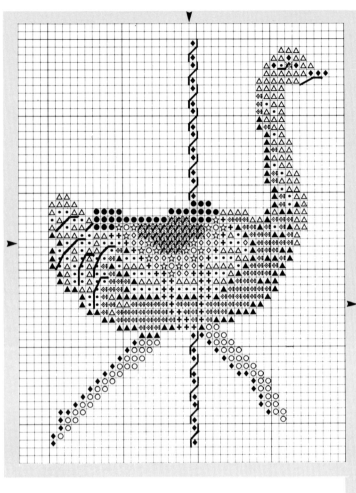

Ostrich

design area 38 sts wide × 53 sts high

Color Key

•	= white	△	= 827 lt blue
☆	= 893 pink	⊗	= 996 med blue
●	= 947 orange	▲	= 824 dk blue
○	= 743 yellow	+	= 552 purple
◆	= 680 gold	✗	= 898 brown
◇	= 701 green		

backstitch tail feathers, med blue; eye, beak and pole, brown

Horse

design area 42 sts wide × 49 sts high

Color Key

•	= white	⊗	= 996 med blue
☆	= 893 pink	+	= 552 purple
●	= 947 orange	□	= 451 gray
○	= 743 yellow	✗	= 898 brown
◆	= 680 gold		
◇	= 701 green		

backstitch eye and pole, brown

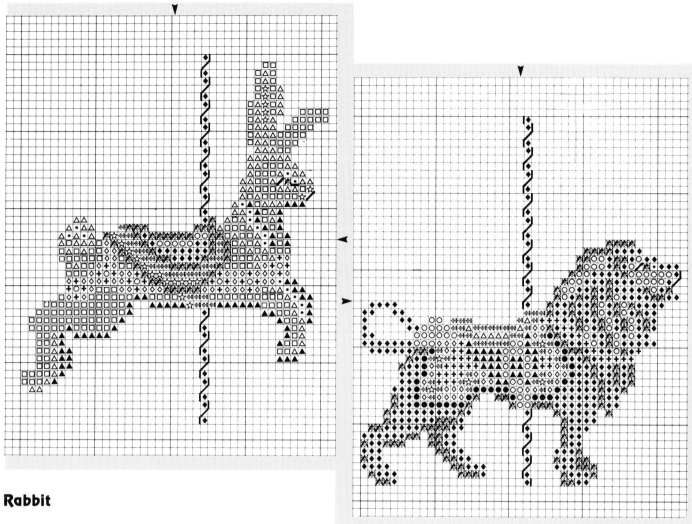

Rabbit

design area 41 sts wide × 48 sts high

Color Key

- • = white
- ☆ = 893 pink
- ○ = 743 yellow
- ◆ = 680 gold
- ◇ = 701 green
- △ = 827 lt blue
- ⊗ = 996 med blue
- ▲ = 824 dk blue
- + = 552 purple
- □ = 451 gray
- ✖ = 898 brown

Lion

design area 43 sts wide × 48 sts high

Color Key

- • = white
- ☆ = 893 pink
- ● = 947 orange
- ○ = 743 yellow
- ◆ = 680 gold
- ◇ = 701 green
- △ = 827 lt blue
- ⊗ = 996 med blue
- ▲ = 824 dk blue
- + = 552 purple
- ✖ = 898 brown

backstitch eye, mouth and pole, brown

Instructions for Making Sampler

Our "Heirloom Sampler" was stitched on 14 count ivory Aida cloth using the 9 designs to fill the 12 spaces. Sampler diagram shows suggested placement of the 9 designs. You may rearrange these designs or change the "Home Sweet Home" to a different message using the Alphabets on pages 8 and 9.

To stitch the Sampler as photographed on the back cover, you will need the following embroidery floss colors:

742 gold	894 pink
422 tan	349 red
700 dk green	517 dk blue
704 lt green	813 lt blue
310 black	433 brown

First the vertical and horizontal rows of cross stitches are worked with 742 gold, leaving 54 squares of fabric between each row. See diagram below. The designs are centered in the spaces after stitching these vertical and horizontal rows. Note that the center of each design is marked on the outside edge of its chart.

The completed Sampler was finished in a 14" × 18" frame. See "Finishing Cross Stitch for Framing," page 17. Each of the 9 designs can also be used on its own and finished in a small frame, hoop or mini pillow. See "Finishing Instructions," page 17.

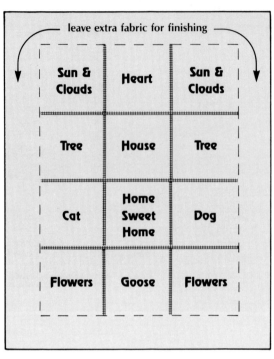

54 squares between stitched rows

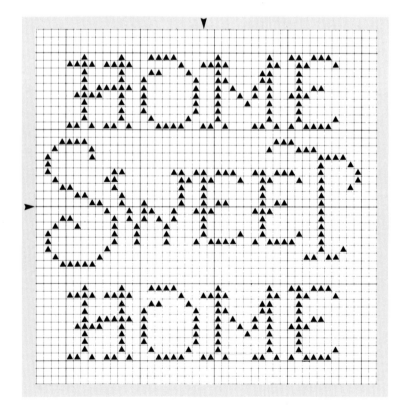

Home Sweet Home

design area 43 sts wide × 40 sts high

Color Key

▲ = 517 dk blue

The "Home Sweet Home," as photographed on the back cover, was stitched on 14 count ivory Aida cloth and finished in a 5" embroidery hoop. See "Finishing Cross Stitch in Hoop," page 17.

Cat

design area 34 sts wide × 41 sts high

Color Key

•	= 742 gold	★	= 349 red
○	= 422 tan	☆	= 894 pink
◆	= 700 dk green	▲	= 517 dk blue
✖	= 310 black		

The "Cat," as photographed on the back cover, was stitched on 14 count ivory Aida cloth and finished in a 4" × 5" frame. See "Finishing Cross Stitch for Framing," page 17.

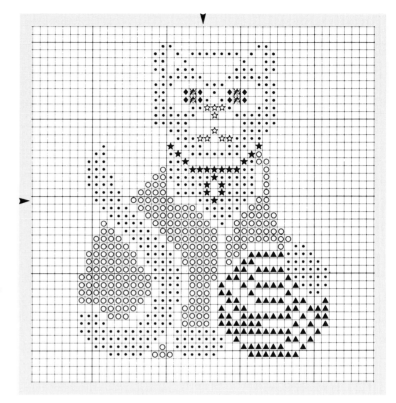

Dog

design area 40 sts wide × 40 sts high

Color Key

○	= 422 tan	☆	= 894 pink
◆	= 700 dk green	▲	= 517 dk blue
✖	= 310 black	◈	= 433 brown

The "Dog," as photographed on the back cover, was stitched on 14 count ivory Aida cloth and finished in a 4" × 5" frame. See "Finishing Cross Stitch for Framing," page 17.

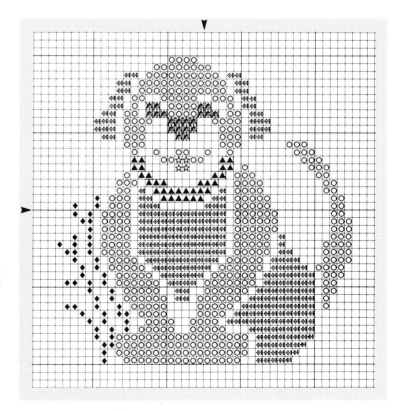

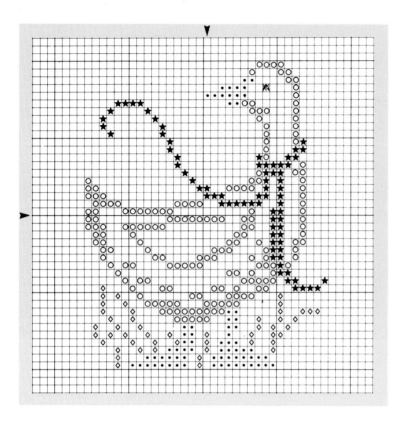

Goose

design area 33 sts wide × 40 sts high

Color Key

○ = 422 tan ◇ = 704 lt green
• = 742 gold ✗ = 310 black
★ = 349 red

The "Goose," as photographed on the back cover, was stitched on 14 count ivory Aida cloth and finished in a 4" × 5" frame. See "Finishing Cross Stitch for Framing," page 17.

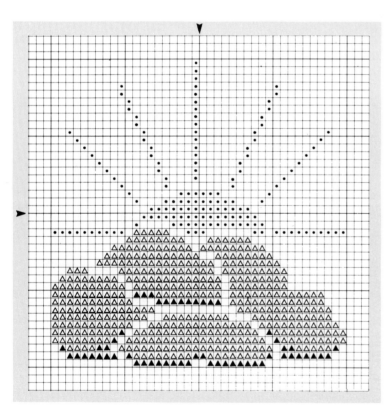

Sun & Clouds

design area 40 sts wide × 39 sts high

Color Key

▲ = 517 dk blue
• = 742 gold
△ = 813 lt blue

House

design area 42 sts wide × 40 sts high

Color Key

○ = 422 tan   △ = 813 lt blue

★ = 349 red   ◆ = 700 dk green

▲ = 517 dk blue   ✗ = 310 black

The "House," as photographed on the back cover, was stitched on 14 count ivory Aida cloth and finished in a 5" embroidery hoop. See "Finishing Cross Stitch in Hoop," page 17.

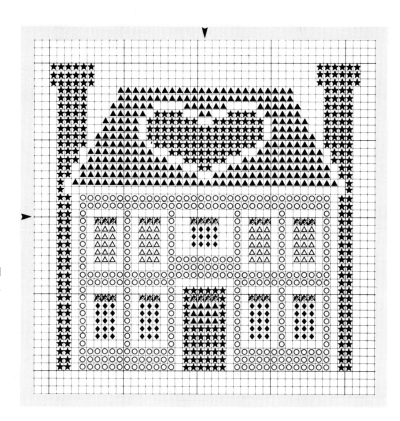

Tree

design area 38 sts wide × 40 sts high

Color Key

◆ = 700 dk green

◇ = 704 lt green

✗ = 433 brown

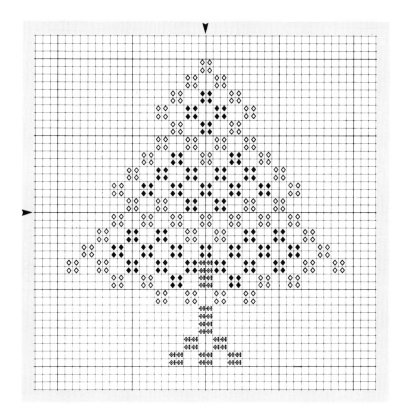

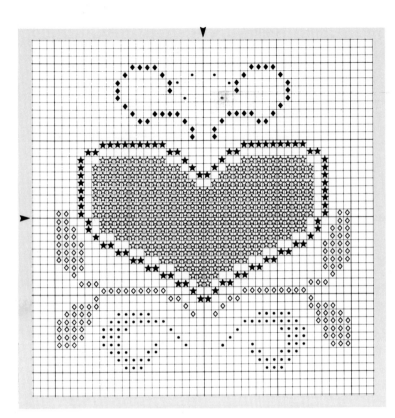

Heart

design area 40 sts wide × 40 sts high

Color Key

★ = 349 red   ◇ = 704 lt green
☆ = 894 pink   • = 742 gold
◆ = 700 dk green

The "Heart," as photographed on the back cover, was stitched on 14 count ivory Aida cloth and finished in a 5" embroidery hoop. See "Finishing Cross Stitch in Hoop," page 17.

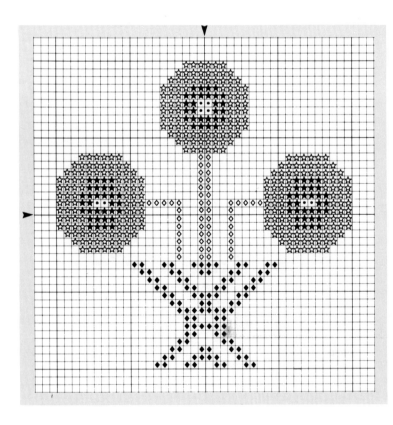

Flowers

design area 40 sts wide × 40 sts high

Color Key

★ = 349 red   ◇ = 704 lt green
☆ = 894 pink   • = 742 gold
◆ = 700 dk green

The "Flowers," as photographed on the back cover, were stitched on 14 count ivory Aida cloth and finished as a 4½" mini pillow. See "Finishing Cross Stitch Pillow or Sachet," page 17.